WHO LIVES HERE?

DESERTS

Mary-Jane Wilkins

BROWN BEAR BOOKS

Published by Brown Bear Books Ltd
4877 N. Circulo Bujia
Tucson, AZ 85718
USA

and

First Floor
9–17 St Albans Place
London N1 0NX

ISBN 978-1-78121-346-9

Library of Congress Cataloging-in-Publication Data available on request

Picture Researcher: Clare Newman
Designer: Melissa Roskell
Design Manager: Keith Davis
Editorial Director: Lindsey Lowe
Children's Publisher: Anne O'Daly

Printed in China

Picture Credits
The photographs in this book are used by permission and through the courtesy of:

Front Cover: Shutterstock: Aaron Amat br, AP Design main, Bandurka tl, Hagit Berkovich cl, Somyot Pannan tlu, Stuart G Porter bl;
Inside: 1, ©Shutterstock/Nataliya Hora; 4, ©Shutterstock/Incredible Arctic; 5, ©iStock/More ISO; 6, ©Shutterstock/Maxim Petrichuk; 6-7, ©Shutterstock/Pichugin Dmitry; 7, ©Shutterstock/Schankz; 8, ©Thinkstock/Vitaani/iStock; 8-9, ©Shutterstock/Aita Oosthuizen; 10, ©Shutterstock/Michel Piccaya; 10-11 ©Photoshot/Joe McDonald/Woodfall Wild Images; 12, ©Shutterstock/Belizar; 13, ©Shutterstock/Johanna Rald/iStock; 14, ©Shutterstock/Hagit Berkovich; 14-15, ©Nature PL/Bruno D/Amicis; 16, ©Thinkstock/Roger de Montfort; 16-17, ©Photoshot/Martin Harvey/NHPA; 18, ©Photoshot/Liu Jian/Xinhua; 18-19, ©Nature PL/Roland Seitre; 20, ©Shutterstock/Wonder Island; 20-21, ©Shutterstock/Volodymyr Burdiak; 22, ©Shutterstock/Tobkatrina; 23, ©Thinkstock/Michak Lootwijk.
T=Top, C=Center, B=Bottom, L=Left, R=Right, U=Upper

Brown Bear Books has made every attempt to contact the copyright holder. If you have any information please contact:
licensing@brownbearbooks.co.uk

CONTENTS

Where Are the DESERTS?

There are deserts all around the world. There are hot deserts and cold deserts. They are all very dry places.

The **biggest** desert is Antarctica. In this cold desert rain falls as snow. Less than 2 inches (5 cm) falls every year.

WOW!

The **biggest** hot desert is the Sahara in North Africa. This has just under 1 inch (2.5 cm) of rain every year.

Animals in deserts have very little water to drink. The biggest desert animals are camels. They can go without water for a long time. You can find out about them and other desert animals in this book.

CAMELS

Most camels are dromedaries. They have one hump on their back and live in Africa and the Middle East.

Another type of camel has two **humps**. These are called Bactrian camels. They live in Asia.

Camels have two rows of long eyelashes to keep sand out of their eyes. They can close their nostrils in a sandstorm.

Camels have very **wide** feet so they can walk over sand without sinking.

MEERKAT

Meerkats are the same size as squirrels. They live in **big** groups in Southern Africa.

Meerkats eat insects, lizards, eggs, and fruit.

Sometimes meerkats stand on their back legs. They look out for predators that might eat them. A hawk or eagle could fly down and ***snatch*** them.

When a meerkat sees a bird, it gives a warning cry. All the meerkats scurry to their burrows.

CARACAL

This wild cat can go for a long time without a drink. It rests during the hottest part of the day. In the early morning or cool evening it hunts birds and small animals.

Big ears help a caracal hear very well.

These cats are amazing **jumpers**. They can knock a bird out of the air 10 feet (3 m) above them. They run ***very fast*** and can catch prey three times their size.

ARMADILLO LIZARD

The armadillo lizard lives in the desert in Southern Africa. It has **tough**, brownish outer skin. This helps it hide in the desert sand. This lizard eats termites and other insects as well as plants.

If an animal attacks, the lizard rolls into a ball. Only the tough outer skin shows.

The thorny devil has scaly skin and sharp **spikes**. They stop animals eating it.

THORNY DEVIL

This small lizard lives in Australia. It walks under wet plants so water drips on its scales. The water runs down the lizard's body and into its mouth.

FENNEC FOX

The fennec fox is small, but it has **huge** ears. It is only 8 inches (20 cm) tall, but its ears can be 6 inches (15 cm) long. Big ears mean that the fox can hear very well.

The fennec fox's big ears help to keep it cool.

Fennec foxes hunt at night when it is cool. They eat beetles and other insects, lizards, and birds.

SIDEWINDER

This snake moves sideways over hot sand. Only two small parts of its body touch the sand as it moves. This stops the snake getting too hot.

Sidewinders are the same color as the sand they hide in.

Sidewinders are predators. They eat lizards and birds. They lie in wait for their prey. The snake buries its body under the sand. Just its head shows. If a lizard comes near, it ***grabs*** and swallows it.

JERBOA

This tiny mouse has very **long** back legs. These help it to hop, just like a kangaroo.

WOW!

This little mouse may never drink. It gets all the water it needs from the food it eats.

A jerboa can jump 9 feet (3 m) when it is trying to get away from a snake or bird that wants to eat it.

TERMITES

These insects build **giant** mounds. Under each mound is a nest. Here the queen termite lays her eggs. Termites eat dead plants and wood. Lizards, snakes, and birds eat termites.

WOW!

Termite nests can hold 20 million insects. The queen is the biggest. She can be 4 inches (10 cm) long.

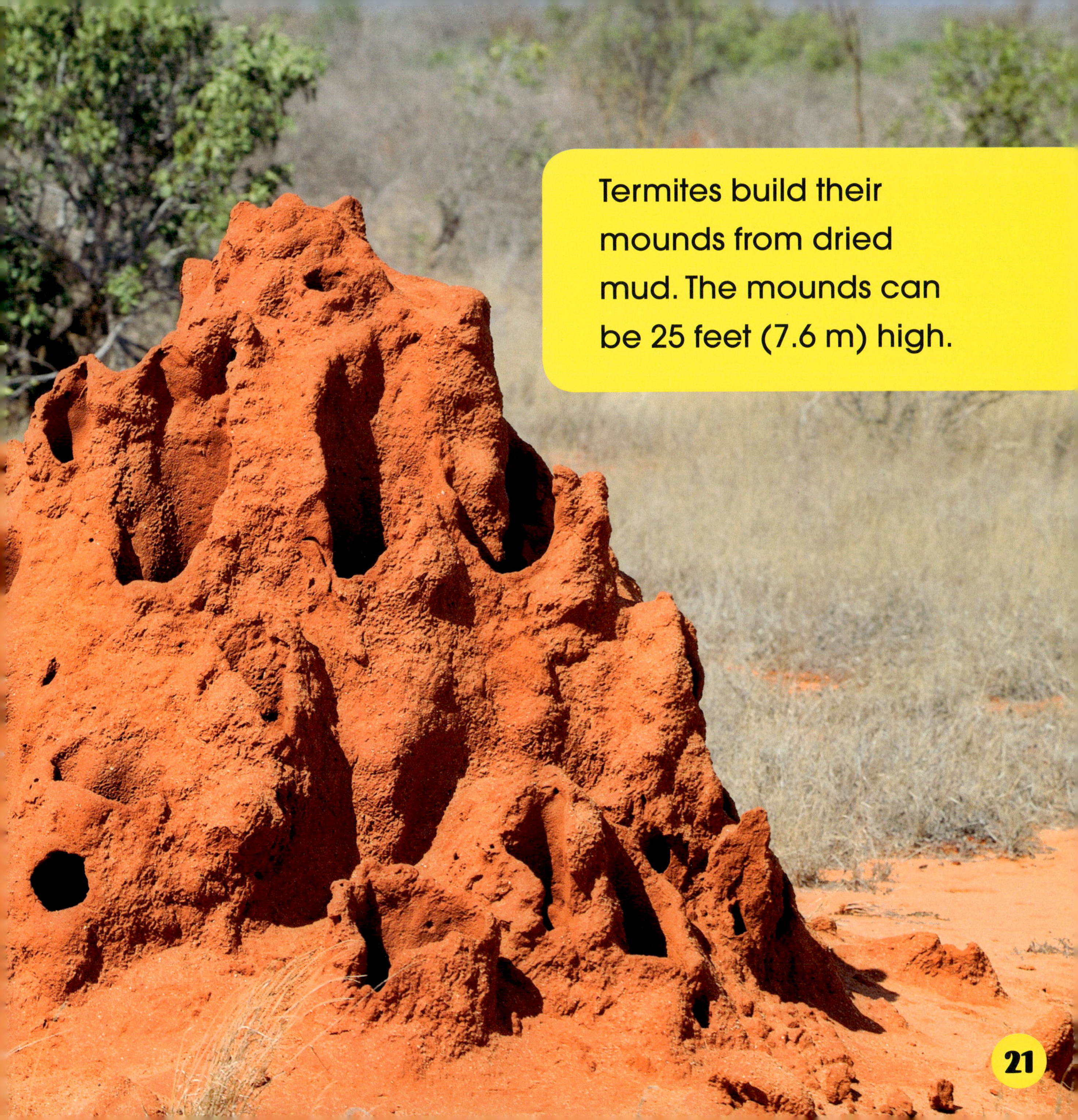

Termites build their mounds from dried mud. The mounds can be 25 feet (7.6 m) high.

DESERT FACTS

Hot deserts are dry, but not hot all the time. At night the temperature can drop to 32°F (0°C).

The hottest place in North America is called Death Valley. It is in the Mojave Desert in California. Here it can be 134°F (57°C) in the summer.

The driest place on Earth is the Atacama Desert. It is in South America. No rain fell on parts of the Atacama Desert for 420 years.

USEFUL WORDS

burrow
An underground home dug by an animal.

predator
An animal that hunts and kills other animals for food. The sidewinder is a predator.

prey
An animal hunted and eaten by another animal. Lizards are the prey of a sidewinder.

scales
The tough layer on the outside of a lizard or snake. Scales protect the animal.

FIND OUT MORE

Deserts Around the World series
Crabtree, 2012

Discover Science: Desert
Nicola Davies, Kingfisher, 2012

Exploring Deserts
Anita Ganeri, Raintree, 2015

Life Cycles: Desert Sean Callery,
Kingfisher, 2013

INDEX